THE FIELDSTONE ALLIANCE NONPROFIT GUIDE TO

Crafting Effective Mission and Vision Statements

THE FIELDSTONE ALLIANCE NONPROFIT GUIDE TO

Crafting Effective Mission and Vision Statements

Emil Angelica

FIELDSTONE
ALLIANCE

SAINT PAUL
MINNESOTA

We thank The David and Lucile Packard Foundation and
the Amherst H. Wilder Foundation for support of this publication.

Edited by Vincent Hyman and Dale S. Thompson
Illustrations and book design by Rebecca Andrews

Manufactured in the United States of America
Third printing, January 2008

The publisher wishes to thank the people who participated in the field test review of this book:

Bryan Barry	Pixie Martin
Lesley Blicker	Pat Peterson
Maricarmen Cortes	Judy Sharken Simon
Paul Fate	Karen Simmons
Peggy Futch	Larry Sommer
Linda Hoskins	Yorn Yan

Library of Congress Cataloging-in-Publication Data

Angelica, Emil, 1946-
   The Wilder nonprofit field guide to crafting effective mission and vision statements / by Emil Angelica.
      p. cm.
   Includes bibliographical references.
   ISBN-13: 978-0-940069-27-5
   ISBN-10: 0-940069-27-X (pbk.)
   1. Mission statements. I. Amherst H. Wilder Foundation.
II. Title.

HD30.285 .A54   2001
658.4'012--dc21   2001003263

To MIPPERS, the little "bird" who has stuck with me for over 35 years.

About the Author

EMIL W. ANGELICA, M.B.A., is president of the Community Consulting Group in Minneapolis, Minnesota. He was a principal consultant with the Wilder Foundation's Center for Communities for more than eighteen years. He has more than twenty-five years experience in providing consulting and training services in the topics of board and staff development, strategic planning, forming alliances, policy and community development, and nonprofit management. He has worked on a broad range of mergers, collaborations, and projects for refugee and immigrant communities. He is known as a national speaker and trainer. In 1998-99 he was commissioned as a Fulbright Scholar in Cyprus. He has published several articles on nonprofit funding issues and has conducted workshops and keynotes on a variety of nonprofit topics. He is coauthor of *Coping with Cutbacks: The Nonprofit Guide to Success When Times Are Tight,* also published by Fieldstone Alliance (formerly Wilder Publishing Center). Emil earned his M.B.A in finance and management from New York University.

Acknowledgments

Many people helped me bring this book to life.

Thanks to Vince Hyman for encouraging, supporting, and threatening me until I put fingers to keyboard; to Becky Andrews for her design skills and the special character of her humor and drawings; and to Dale Thompson for a first-class editing job that made my thinking understandable.

Special thanks to my colleagues at Wilder Foundation, who taught me much and gave me their professional expertise when needed. In particular, thanks to Bryan Barry, Carol Lukas, and Judy Sharken Simon, with whom I have worked for fifteen years.

Thanks to Jean Wieger, who taught me about intuition and how to access its power.

Thanks to the following individuals and organizations who contributed examples to this book—Kimberly Anderson, Executive Director, National Association for the Mentally Ill–Minnesota Chapter; Lawrence H. Borom, President/CEO, The City, Inc.; Claudia Dengler, Vice President, Services to Children, Elderly, and Families, Amherst H. Wilder Foundation; William R. King, Senior Vice President, Minnesota Council on Foundations; Eric Stevens, Executive Director, Courage Center.

Thanks to the book review team—Bryan Barry, Lesley Blicker, Maricarmen Cortes, Paul Fate, Peggy Futch, Linda Hoskins, Pixie Martin, Pat Peterson, Judy Sharken Simon, Karen Simmons, Larry Sommer, and Yorn Yan—who gave their attention to reviewing drafts of this book and whose comments and critiques enabled me to strengthen it.

And finally, thanks to my wife, Marion, who has supported all my endeavors for thirty-five years and believes in me; and my son, Ethan, and daughter, Carmen, who sharpen my management and observation skills and provide me with a wealth of stories.

Contents

Why Mission and Vision Statements Are So Important: Opportunities Lost...*and Gained*

"C'mon, put some muscle into it...we're not getting anywhere!"

AS A CONSULTANT to nonprofit organizations I often begin my work with an organization by asking to see the current mission and vision statements. The response can give me a pretty clear picture of how the organization functions. On one such occasion, I was working with an organization that was having significant financial problems, and within a day it was easy to see why. In individual interviews, I asked board members and staff from throughout the organization to tell me the organization's mission and vision for the future. Each person I spoke with had a different take on where the organization was going.

This organization faced the three typical problems experienced by organizations that lack visible, well-defined mission and vision statements:

- *Disjointed and competing programs.* Since program managers each acted on their own version of the organization's mission and vision for the future, programs had developed in a scattered way and were disconnected from each other. There were instances where programs were actually working on competing outcomes for customers.

- *Decreased funding.* In the absence of clear statements of a desired future, the staff had resorted to chasing dollars to fund programs and services. Programs and services were developed based on the funders' goals rather than the organization's mission and vision. Eventually funders and donors realized what was happening, and support to the organization declined.

- *Poor decision-making.* Without having a working mission or vision statement that they had agreed to, board members had nothing to anchor decisions on. When the staff and community asked board members to make choices, they were at a loss because one option appeared to be as good as another. The board fell down on its responsibility to focus the organization and its work.

Because this organization had no clearly defined and agreed-to mission and vision statements, it was adrift at sea, in significant financial trouble, unable to make a consistent, positive impact on the community, and without any guide to get it back on course.

Compare this to a social service organization of similar size that had spent significant time preparing its mission and vision statements and building ownership for them by involving board and staff in their development. When I conducted interviews, everyone defined the desired future in the same way. This common understanding of the organization supported three critical outcomes:

- *Unified and compatible services.* In making decisions to contract or expand services, program staff looked first at how well the services fit with the mission and vision statements and then on need and available funding. This led to compatible services that accomplished more together than they could have alone.

- *Increased funding.* Funders grew to understand clearly what the organization was about and were impressed with its consistent approach to new program development and its focused plan for serving the community. Foundations and donors wanted to be part of this success.

- *Solid decision-making and rewarding collaborations.* The board felt good about the organization because it could readily describe its purpose and role in the community. Decision-making had a solid connection to the community and the future. An added benefit was that the leadership could more easily collaborate with other organizations because it could identify organizations with similar goals for the future, clarify what it needed to get out of any joint effort, and create mission and vision statements for the collaboration.

These two examples show that the difference is dramatic when everyone involved with an organization knows the organization's purpose and future direction. A well-crafted mission statement helps an organization stay focused by clearly stating what business the organization is in. Similarly, an effective vision statement keeps the organization moving by describing the organization's desired future.

This booklet will help your organization create (or revise) mission and vision statements that bring focus and direction to your work.

How to Use This Guide

To help your organization develop mission and vision statements, I have created this brief how-to guide that outlines orderly, easy-to-follow steps that any nonprofit can use to write effective mission and vision statements. The guide is divided into four sections:

Part I defines mission and vision statements, distinguishes between them, and tells you how to use both for the maximum benefit of your organization.

Part II outlines a seven-step process for developing a mission statement that captures exactly what your organization does, provides a lasting challenge to all involved in the organization's work, and distinguishes your organization from all others. Though the general approach presented is the same for all organizations, the statement your organization produces will be unique.

Part III presents a six-step process that shows you how to use stakeholders' ideas and your organization's history, capacity for growth, and fundraising potential as the cornerstone of the visioning process. It also gives you four options for developing a vision of your organization's short-term future. The six-step process, along with the mission statement process, increases the leadership effectiveness of those who participate in it.

The *Appendix* includes worksheets to guide participants through the creation of mission and vision statements.

You can use this guide to craft a mission statement, a vision statement, or both. If your organization is creating a mission statement and vision statement for the first time, we suggest you conduct a strategic planning process, involve key leaders from the board, staff, and volunteers, and use the approach for creating a mission and vision outlined in this book. Otherwise, use the part of this guide that fits your situation, such as in

- *Routine organizational planning.* Every time you conduct a strategic planning process, use the six-step vision development process. If you plan annually, try employing the different options as outlined in Vision Step 2: Generate Alternative Visions, pages 29-33.

- *Planning that does not change the mission.* Most plans do not change the core mission of the organization, but you can still revisit certain steps for developing a mission statement. Mission Step 2: Clarify Core Values, Step 3: Review the Organization's Underlying Strategies, and Step 4: Evaluate the Current Mission Statement (pages 18-21) help you think about the future.

- *Planning that does change the mission statement.* If you believe that you will need to revise your mission statement, state this up front. Make it a major part of your planning process and follow the seven steps for creating a mission statement.

A cautionary note: Change the mission statement only when significant change seems necessary. The mission is important to the organization's identity and actions; it should remain constant for many years. It is often part of an organization's articles of incorporation. Therefore, once a new mission statement is adopted by the board, the organization may need to refile with the IRS, the state commission on charitable organizations, and other agencies as required by law.

Let's get started!

PART I

Understanding and Using Mission and Vision Statements

I BELIEVE THAT a good *mission statement* is a short, snappy statement of the purpose of the organization, capable of fitting at the bottom of the organization's letterhead or business card. As John Carver[1] says, it should answer the question, "What good, for whom?" It needs to be so memorable that it flows easily off the tongues of board, staff, and volunteers. Everyone committed to the organization should know the mission statement by heart because it is the reason the organization exists and is the basis of people's commitment to the organization. It should be free of jargon and so clear that the average person will understand it without further explanation or definition. Here are examples of mission statements developed by nonprofit organizations I have worked with:

- Ensure that all people with developmental disabilities have full access to their civil, legal, and human rights.

- Improve communities and support the self-sufficiency of low- and moderate-income families.

---

[1] John Carver is an internationally known consultant and author and the principal in Carver Governance Design, Inc., which works with nonprofit organizations on governance and the board-executive partnership.

- Create affordable housing for St. Paul's core neighborhoods.
- Promote the social welfare of people in the metropolitan area.

Though brief, the mission statement must possess four important qualities: breadth, durability, challenge, and distinction. The mission statement must be broad because it is an umbrella statement that encompasses all of the organization's programs and services. It must be long lasting, setting the organization's direction for the next twenty years. It also should pose a continuing challenge to board, staff, and volunteers, guiding the outcomes and the means (the *what* and the *how*) of the work to be done. Courage Center, a large provider of services to people with disabilities, has written challenge right into its mission statement with these words: "to empower people with disabilities to reach for their full potential in every aspect of life. We are guided by our vision that one day all people will live, work, learn, and play in a community based on abilities, not disabilities." It is clear that if the center's programs and services are not empowering people, then Courage Center is failing at its job. The challenge lies in enabling customers to achieve "full potential" and to do so in "every aspect of life."

Though brief, the mission statement must possess four important qualities: breadth, durability, challenge, and distinction.

Finally, a mission statement should separate your organization from the rest of the pack by distinguishing its work from the work of similar organizations. For example, the mission statement of the Minnesota Council on Foundations differentiates its work from that of other philanthropic organizations by emphasizing that its goal is "to strengthen and increase participation in organized philanthropy." Unlike similar organizations it is not trying to increase the general public's individual giving. Instead, its aim is to encourage and enable wealthy individuals to establish foundations that will increase institutional giving.

It is important to point out that I have a bias toward short, memorable mission statements. Not all people agree with me. The steps in this guide will help you create such a mission statement. To keep it brief, you will need to free the mission statement from statements of values and descriptions of strategies. This can be done by spending time identifying the organization's core values and underlying strategies *before* writing or revising the mission statement.

Values and strategies are at the core of the organization. They are understood intuitively by the board and staff. By uncovering these first, the people working on the mission statement are free to develop one that embodies the spirit of those values and strategies without listing them.

For balance, here is a mission statement that *does* include values and strategies statements

> *National Association for the Mentally Ill–Minnesota Chapter champions justice, dignity, and respect for all people affected by mental illness (biological brain disorders). Through education, advocacy, and support, we strive to eliminate the pervasive stigma of mental illness, effect positive changes in the mental health system, and increase the public and professional understanding of mental illness.*

This organization is just as effective at achieving its mission as the previous organizations. While its mission statement is not as easy to remember as the previous examples, it does make clear the overall mission, some of the strategies by which the mission will be accomplished, and the values that shape the organization's approach.

The *vision statement* sketches a picture of the organization's desired future in a few paragraphs. It answers two questions: "What will be different in the world in three to five years because our organization exists? And, what role will our organization play in creating that difference?" The answer to these questions should be broad outcome statements rather than a list of the organization's activities. The outcome statements outline what the organization is attempting to achieve and the general role it will play in moving toward its vision. Here are some examples of outcome statements that might be included in a vision statement:

> A good vision statement inspires and challenges the board, staff, and volunteers without overwhelming them—they must believe they can accomplish it.

- Change the health and human service delivery systems so that people with disabilities do not face additional barriers when compared to other customers being served by the system.
- Recognize, eliminate, and prevent racism in philanthropy.
- Eliminate cultural and economic barriers so that all young people can achieve success in education.

A good vision statement inspires and challenges the board, staff, and volunteers without overwhelming them—they must believe they can accomplish it. A three-to-five-year time frame achieves this balance; it is far enough into the future that people can envision change happening but is not so far that *anything* seems possible. For most organizations, a three-to-five-year time frame corresponds with three to five budget cycles.

Following are two excerpts from vision statements. A third example may be found in Figure 1. This example, a poem, shows the kinds of creativity that can be applied to vision statements.

- The Wilder Foundation's vision is a vibrant St. Paul, where individuals, families, and communities can prosper, with opportunities for all to be employed, to be engaged citizens, to live in decent housing, to attend good schools, and to receive support during times of need.

- It is envisioned that by 1997 The City, Inc., will be helping approximately 3,000 inner-city young people and families improve their lives. As a result of the labors of a staff that is better trained and better educated than ever before, it is hoped that the inner-city people served by The City will have more hope, greater work skill levels, more opportunities for advancement, both socially and in the workplace, and that their communities will be stronger. Further, it is envisioned that The City will reinforce its reputation as an agency that administers effective, well-supervised and culturally appropriate programs that result not only in personal growth but in a collective strengthening of the communities served for more than a quarter of a century. The City will forge many partnerships and linkages with people and organizations to achieve our goals. Staff will be highly motivated, well-trained, eager to learn and serve and will have concern for empowering our communities and the young people and families that reside here.

Figure 1: You can be creative in a vision statement!

Vision statements can and should inspire by painting a picture of the future as shaped by your organization's efforts. This vision for the Minnesota Council on Foundations was written as a poem by Pat Cummings, one of its board members.

We stand together on the bank of the river,
    Scanning the twin landscapes of space and time,

        We seek a vision,
            And find it
            Rising out of our past,
            Reflecting our interior landscapes,
            Responding to the exterior.

And we see, on the other side of the river…
    …A new and larger landscape with new forms joining old,
        To create a balanced whole,
        Circling a common mission,
        Encompassing common values;
        But, leaving room for each of us to celebrate
        Our unique spirits.

    …An inclusive environment,
        Harnessing the power of our diversity
        To drive us forward with new energy;
        Recognizing dark and light,
        Each and all committed to works of excellence.

    …A place of many paths,
        Challenging us to step out as leaders
        Into uncharted territories;
        Where we support each other when risks are great,
        Trusting that even hidden paths can lead us to the same destination.

    …A structure, solidly grounded, yet rising high,
        In which the cornerstone of ethics,
        And the keystone of creativity,
        Support space for all voices,
        Within a sound framework.

    …An evolutionary community, always transformative,
        Where we continue to seek new understandings,
        To nurture new generations;
        Reaching beyond our own landscape
        To form new alliances,
        To share who we are and what we know.

    …A new horizon,
        Bounded only by the limits we may set for ourselves,
        As we focus on the *why* of what we do.

Vision statements are typically longer than mission statements, and may be several paragraphs.

Every member of the organization should be able to make a connection between her or his daily activities and the organization's vision statement. To see if a connection exists, I often ask line staff these questions:

- What is your organization's vision?
- How does it affect your customers?
- How does your job support the vision?

In one organization, the receptionist for the jobs program understood that part of the organization's vision was to ensure that people with disabilities got good paying jobs. She directly connected this part of the vision to the program in which she worked. In her job as receptionist, meeting customers and talking with them over the phone, she came to realize how important employment was for them. She also recognized that her job was pivotal in connecting customers with program staff who could help them get jobs. As the receptionist she understood that *she was the organization* for the people who called for the first time and that her understanding of the organization and its programs and services was important in quickly and effectively connecting callers to a person who could help them.

Though the vision statement gives the organization direction, the leadership should regard it as written in pencil. External factors such as welfare reform, a booming economy, and low unemployment can affect the role an organization plays in its community. Leaders should not be afraid to change the vision statement as circumstances change—remembering as they do so that the organization exists for the good of its community.

"I'm supporting the town's vision of being
a vibrant, non-flooded place to live."

How Mission and Vision Work Together

Based on these definitions, the vision statement fits under the umbrella of the mission statement. The organization's leaders must own both the vision and mission statements and be able to explain them easily in any venue.[2]

There is an important relationship between planning, decision-making, mission, and vision. Most organizations conduct a strategic planning process to revisit their existing mission statement and to decide whether it needs to be updated. At that time, they may also develop a vision statement to describe the desired outcome of their plan. Some boards regularly review their organization's mission and vision statements as they monitor its work and evaluate the performance against the desired outcomes. Finally, some boards address the mission statement as they develop policy statements that direct the work of staff and volunteers.

So, when and how does this planning occur? When should the steps described in this guide be applied? Many organizations review their strategic plan annually, and this is a good time to review and, if appropriate, change mission, vision, or both. Here are three scenarios in which this usually occurs:

- *Modified review.* The board holds a meeting to review and, if necessary, update mission and vision statements. It may do this in place of a full-scale planning process. In this case, the board is the planning group and a subset of the group is the writing team. (Both of these groups are referred to as you progress through the steps in this booklet.) This might call for one board meeting to review and comment on the mission and vision statements, and one or more board meetings of the writing team to craft the changes. Finally, the writing team presents the revised statements to the board for approval and adoption or modification and further revision.

- *Full-scale planning.* The board, key staff, and volunteers embark on a major strategic planning process. Everyone who participates constitutes the planning group. An outside consultant often facilitates the planning. Usually, the strategic planning includes steps for data collection, idea generation, and plan development. During data gathering, customers, clients, funders, policy

---

[2] Some current literature on mission and vision statements defines them differently than I have; in fact, some writers define them in exactly the opposite way. The definitions I've given, however, are consistent with the most common usage and with Fieldstone Alliance's publications on strategic planning and marketing.

makers, staff, volunteers, competitors, and other stakeholders contribute information. During idea generation, the planning group develops themes from the data, and notes which themes should be incorporated into the strategic plan, including mission or vision statements. Finally, during plan development, a subset of the planning group drafts the plan, mission, and vision. Eventually, the board approves the entire plan, along with the new or revised mission and vision.

- *Large organization planning.* In some cases—usually in larger organizations—the board may appoint a committee to do the planning. This committee is the planning group, and it will select a writing team (or a single writer) to revise the mission and vision according to the direction of the planning group. Depending on the depth of the planning, the committee may follow the approach described for a modified review, or it may follow that for full-scale planning. Regardless, the mission and vision need to go before the board for approval once the committee work is complete.

The act of revisiting mission and vision—even when conducted with no other type of planning or review—usually unearths important strategic questions.

The point is that revising (or creating for the first time) a mission statement, vision statement, or both usually happens as a part of some larger organizational process. In fact, the act of revisiting mission and vision—even when conducted with no other type of planning or review—usually unearths important strategic questions. If you are using this booklet, you are likely involved in some broader planning process. The steps in this booklet, however, are designed so that they can be carried on either isolated from *or* in conjunction with other processes. In other words, you can write only a mission statement, only a vision statement, or both, but not take on a strategic plan—or you can conduct all three. Keep in mind that if you are involved in a more significant plan, some of the steps herein will need to be modified as you incorporate them in the larger planning effort.

Using Mission and Vision Statements

An organization can use its mission and vision statements in many ways. For example, both can play a prominent role in framing the organization during the orientation and development of the board, staff, and volunteers. Following are specific ways each statement can be used.

Ways to use the mission statement

Brief, clear, and memorable, the mission statement should become synonymous with the organization's name. Here are some suggestions for getting the most mileage from this powerful statement.

- *Planning.* To be sure that plans are on the right track, refer to your mission statement early and often during all planning processes. For example, post the mission on newsprint at all planning meetings, and include the mission in summaries for those meetings.

- *Customer service.* To make clients feel at home, display the statement in service areas in their language(s) as well as in English; also, make the statement readily available in your administrative and executive offices. For example, put it on mouse pads, printed forms, internal phone directories, and other places where it's likely to be seen often.

- *Marketing.* To ensure that you represent your organization clearly, correctly, and positively at all times, distribute the statement throughout all marketing and general information materials and on the first page of the strategic plan and annual report. For example, include it on newsletters, business cards, holiday greeting cards, and brochures.

- *Fundraising.* To add punch to applications and requests for funding, include your mission statement; its clarity and breadth of vision will make a strong impression on all who read it. For example, include it on thank you notes, funding reports, and letters of inquiry.

"Oh my, there's that mission statement again!"

Ways to use the vision statement

The essence of the vision statement is that it defines the outcomes that are the focus of your organization's work. Because of this, it should appear as the directional statement in the organization's strategic plan and annual report. Here are other effective uses for the vision statement:

- *Aligning.* To make sure that staff and volunteers draw a connection between their work and the organization's broad goals, put the vision statement at the front of staff work plans, where it can't be missed. For example, include a discussion of the vision at employee performance reviews—connect the vision to the employee's role in the organization and even to the employee's professional development plan.

- *Fundraising.* To strengthen fundraising proposals, include the vision statement; it paints a compelling picture of the future the organization is trying to bring about and provides a context within which the requested funding will be used. For example, show how the requested funds will contribute to the future expressed in your vision statement, especially in the outcome statements it includes.

- *Informing.* To keep policy makers and governmental agency officials up to date, you may sometimes want to use the vision statement to sketch a picture of the organization's desired future and to explain a position taken by the organization. For example, an advocacy organization can use its vision statement as a starting point to explain the policy changes necessary to create the desired future.

PART II

Developing the Mission Statement

"They've been in there for hours, but it sounds like they're making real progress..."

"Ok, we agree on the lunch menu, now let's go on to the mission statement."

MANY METHODS can be used to develop a mission statement. The step-by-step process discussed here is a practical approach that I have used successfully with large and small organizations. Its benefit is that it is simple and relatively easy to use with board, staff, and volunteers. Whether your organization is writing its first mission statement or rethinking the current one, this basic seven-step guide can help. Typically, the process can be accomplished in five to fifteen hours. Some organizations hold one meeting per step, while others hold a one to two day retreat during which they craft the mission statement.

Step 1: Select the Mission Statement Writing Team

Typically the board chair appoints a writing team of one to three experienced people to be responsible for participating in the board's planning process and then writing the mission statement.

Step 2: Clarify Core Values

The leadership identifies the priority statements of belief that are the basic building blocks of the organization and that shape the criteria for determining right and wrong within the organization.

Step 3: Review the Organization's Underlying Strategies

The writing team reviews the underlying strategies that the organization uses to achieve its mission. If these have not been stated explicitly, they can be determined by reviewing the organization's programs and services.

Step 4: Evaluate the Current Mission Statement

The board and staff leadership review the current mission statement and critique it. This activity provides the basis for determining if the mission statement needs to be rewritten.

Step 5: Draft the Mission Statement

The mission statement writing team composes or rewrites the mission statement.

Step 6: Circulate the Mission Statement for Review and Modify It

The writing team circulates the draft of the mission statement to key stakeholders for review and comment. The writing team then modifies the mission statement if necessary.

Step 7: Adopt the Mission Statement

The board reviews the mission statement and adopts it for the organization.

For best results, follow the steps in order, omitting none of them. Steps 2, 3, and 4 (the planning steps) make it easier for practical thinkers who are involved in only one phase of the organization to understand and accept the necessarily general ideas the mission statement expresses. Steps 2, 3, and 4 disclose your organization's key values and underlying strategies, giving the writing team the knowledge it needs to write a powerful, precise statement that captures the essence of your organization's work. Do not skip over these steps in your rush to Step 5: Draft the Mission Statement.

Typically Steps 2, 3, and 4 are often done as part of a daylong planning meeting of the board and key staff. If no daylong meeting is planned, schedule two or three planning meetings or complete Steps 2, 3, and 4 during regularly scheduled board meetings. Throughout this booklet, the board and key staff working on the mission statement will be referred to as the planning group. In the appendix you will find worksheets to help you develop your mission statement.

Step 1: Select the Mission Statement Writing Team

Make this critical step the first thing you do rather than an afterthought. In this way everyone will know who is responsible for writing the mission statement from the beginning, and the writing team can gather the information it will need from the start of the process. Typically the board chair appoints a writing team of one to three people. The team may include board and staff; the executive director is often involved. The team should include leaders (formal or informal) who, ideally, have a range of seniority within the organization and can honestly represent the different viewpoints that exist in the organization. All team members must have demonstrated writing ability and a strong commitment to be involved in all phases of the planning process. For some organizations, the most important selection criterion is trust. Where there are differing perspectives, board and staff must trust that the mission statement the writing team develops will reflect the thinking of the entire planning group rather than the team's own perspectives.

Variation to Step 1

Instead of using an in-house writing team, engage a professional writer (a paid or volunteer marketing or writing consultant) who is not a participant in the planning process. The consultant observes the planning process and identifies key ideas and critical words as the planning group discusses various issues. Once the planning is done, the consultant drafts one or more separate statements of values, mission, and underlying strategies and presents them to the planning group for review and comment. Based on the planning group's comments, the consultant then redrafts one statement for values, one for mission, and one for underlying strategies and presents a final version of the mission statement to the board for adoption.

- *Advantages.* The mission statement will be well crafted and written so that it is easily marketable. Also, since the consultant is not a participant, she or he has the luxury of listening to the planning process with only the writing task in mind. Finally, since the writer is an "outsider," people feel more comfortable critiquing and, if necessary, rejecting a draft.

- *Disadvantages.* The planning group may have trouble owning the statement if the consultant chooses not to use the group's words. Also, the statement may seem "slick" and not in keeping with the organization's image. Finally, the planning group may not critically review the consultant's work, believing that a professional knows best. However, a good consultant will be able to overcome most of these problems.

Turn to Mission Worksheet 1: Select the Mission Statement Writing Team, page 43.

Step 2: Clarify Core Values

To be brief and powerful, your mission statement cannot include all of your organization's values and underlying strategies. In developing the mission statement, the planning group will use Step 2: Clarify Core Values and Step 3: Review the Organization's Underlying Strategies to identify the organization's key values and strategies. The writing team will use this information to write a mission statement that is informed by the organization's values and strategies but does not explicitly state them.

Core values are broad, brief statements of belief that shape the criteria by which the board, staff, and volunteers can judge whether or not the stated vision, plans, actions, and outcomes are the right ones for the organization. They are the organization's basic building blocks and the reason board, staff, and volunteers joined the organization; they form the core of the leadership's thinking.

To identify your organization's key values, divide the planning group into small groups of three to six people and have each group appoint a recorder to take notes. Ask each person to take ninety seconds to start an individual list of the core values that are important or basic to the organization and to her or his commitment to the

"Hmmm...maybe 'He who loses buys the beer' belongs on the 'personal values' table."

organization. Keep people working quickly because you want the main values, not a laundry list. If people have too much time they will create a list with every value that they can imagine. As shown in Mission Worksheet 2 and below, values should be specific statements rather than one-word platitudes such as "honest," "trustworthy," "loyal."

Here are some examples of values:
- Women should have equal opportunity in every career field.
- Racism is the major barrier that keeps people from being full participants in our community.
- People with disabilities have the right to participate fully in community life.

Once the individual lists have been completed, have each person share her or his ideas with the small group. The recorder compiles a list of the values that the group agrees to. Each small group's recorder reads the list to the entire planning group. Someone records each small group's list, combining and amending values to avoid duplication. The planning group prioritizes the final list of unduplicated values by having each person cast votes equivalent to one-fourth of the total number of values in the final list. From this, three to six values will clearly stand out as those most important to the planning group. Remember that you are clarifying your values so that they can be stated *separately* from your final mission statement and so that the mission statement will be grounded in them. That way, you can keep your mission statement concise and memorable—embodying your values without making them explicit.

Distribute Mission Worksheet 2: Clarify Core Values, page 45, to participants, small group recorders, or both.

Step 3: Review the Organization's Underlying Strategies

Underlying strategies are the methods (approaches) your organization uses to accomplish its mission. Laid out by the board and key staff, these strategies shape the organization and determine whether it is a direct service provider, an indirect service provider, an advocacy agency, or a combination of these. A list of the underlying strategies establishes the boundaries within which the staff develops programs and services and guides the board in directing the organization's resources. In some instances a list of the underlying strategies already exists, or they may have been developed in one of the previous strategic planning sessions. If not, they are usually reflected in the goals that underlie specific programs or approaches to accomplishing the mission.

Here is an example of three underlying strategies for an organization that works with people who have developmental disabilities:

- Provide education and information about developmental disabilities to policy makers and the public.
- Advocate for the rights of people who are not able to represent themselves because of developmental disabilities.
- Develop high-quality facilities and programs that enable people with developmental disabilities to live independently.

Reviewing the organization's underlying strategies is often (and perhaps best) done as part of a strategic planning process. When this is the case, the board and staff members participating in the strategic planning process develop strategies to accomplish goals or address critical issues. This is usually done either at a retreat or as a part of strategic planning meetings. They may also evaluate current or potential programs and categorize them into broad strategies. The results of either or both activities are then submitted to the mission statement writing team.

If the organization is *not* involved in a strategic planning process, the mission writing team reviews existing programs and strategies and classifies programs into broad strategies following the example for the organization that works with people with developmental disabilities. Remember that you are doing this step to be sure that the mission statement is *grounded in* your current strategies. You will not be incorporating underlying strategies into the mission statement itself.

Turn to Mission Worksheet 3: Review the Organization's Underlying Strategies, page 47, for a guide to reviewing or identifying strategies.

Step 4: Evaluate the Current Mission Statement

Divide the planning group into small groups of three to six people and have each group appoint a recorder to take notes. Ask each person to read the current mission statement and then answer the following questions.

- Is the current mission statement short and snappy? If not, what is the problem?

- Does it tell people what good the organization is doing and for whom? If not, what is missing, or is too much included?

- Is it grounded in our values as clarified in Step 2? If not, what is missing? (Remember, though, that the mission statement should not be a *list* of your values. It needs to capture their essence without being muddied up by a long list.)

- Does the statement serve as an umbrella that covers all the things we do—our underlying strategies as captured in Step 3? If not, what is not included under the umbrella? (Remember, though, that the mission statement should not be a listing of program strategies.)

Frank was a good example of what a mission statement should be—short and snappy.

- Does the statement encompass all the people to whom we target our services? If not, which customers are missing?

- Does the statement communicate who we are to the average person? If not, why not? For example, does it have too much jargon? Is it unclear or too abstract?

- Is this a statement we can get excited about and be proud of? If not, what must be done?

Once everyone in the group has finished, each person shares her or his answers with the small group, while the recorder writes down the answers that the group generally agrees to. After the answers to the questions have been recorded, someone from each group makes a one-minute report to all planning participants. Collect the results and write them up as part of the summary of the meeting.

Distribute Mission Worksheet 4: Evaluate the Current Mission Statement, page 49, to participants, small group recorders, or both.

Step 5: Draft the Mission Statement

The writing team collects the results of the work done in Steps 2, 3, and 4 and summarizes the organization's values, underlying strategies, and current mission statement. This requires generalizing from the specific statements produced by the small groups and prioritizing the values and strategies. The key to writing the mission statement lies in understanding the overall organization, its stakeholders, and its future direction and then writing an umbrella statement that answers the question, "What good, for whom?"

Since the mission statement will be (or should be) the most widely read and used phrase in the organization, it is the hardest single sentence to write. Save this step until the writing team has gained all the knowledge it can about the views of the board and key staff.

Variation to Step 5

At the end of the planning process, involve all participants in the planning process in developing several versions of the mission statement. Divide participants into small groups of three to five, and ask each group to come up with its own draft statements of values, mission, and underlying strategies. To keep people from feeling that they have come up with a finished product, give them no more than an hour to do this. You do not want anyone to have too much at stake in what she or he has written, because the writing team will summarize all the small groups' statements and refine them to produce a single mission statement. This statement goes to the board and staff for review and comment before it is polished and brought to the board for adoption.

> Since the mission statement will be (or should be) the most widely read and used phrase in the organization, it is the hardest single sentence to write. Save this step until the writing team has gained all the knowledge it can about the views of the board and key staff.

- *Advantages.* This approach works best in a government agency program or in an organization that has a small board and limited number of key staff. When the entire planning group helps draft the mission statement, group members more readily own it. They feel connected to it, appreciate the difficulty of the writing task, and understand why certain words have been selected.

- *Disadvantages.* If people in the planning group have significant differences, some may become attached to their version of the draft statement and find it difficult to accept the statement that the writing team develops. Also, if the planning group is large (twenty-five or more people), the process becomes unwieldy. Too many options emerge, making it difficult for the writing team to focus its work.

Distribute Mission Worksheet 5: Draft the Mission Statement, page 53, to the mission statement writing team.

Step 6: Circulate the Mission Statement for Review and Modify It

The writing team circulates the draft mission statement to the planning group, and, if appropriate, board members, staff, volunteers, some customers, and certain informants, such as significant funders and donors, former leaders, key allies, and the like. The writing team asks them to respond to three questions:

- Do you understand the mission statement? If not, explain.
- Does it fit your experiences with our organization? If not, explain.
- Do you like this statement as a mission for our organization? If not, explain.

Once the mission writing team gets answers, it modifies the mission statement and submits it to the board for adoption.

Distribute Mission Worksheet 6: Review and Comment on the Mission Statement, page 55, to the people selected for this task.

Step 7: Adopt the Mission Statement

When submitting the statement to the board, the writing team should also submit a summary of the reviewers' responses. The board formally reviews the statement at a board meeting and considers the summary of responses. If the writing team made significant changes to the last draft, the board discusses them. If the board decides that the statement doesn't meet its standards or reflect the reviewers' feedback, the same or a different writing team further refines the statement and resubmits it to the board.

When the board is satisfied that the statement meets the organization's standard for a mission statement, the board formally adopts it. As quickly as possible the newly adopted mission statement replaces the old one throughout the organization.

Review the mission statement at least once a year to make certain that new board and staff members know and understand it and to ensure that the board and staff continue to support it. Since the mission statement is basic, important, and widely used, the board should be deliberate in making changes. However, if the board and key staff have significant concerns about it, they should open discussions about redrafting it.

PART III

Developing the Vision Statement

YOUR ORGANIZATION may wish to create a new vision statement under any of the following conditions:

- The organization has significantly changed its mission statement.
- The organization has no agreed-on vision for the future.
- The current vision statement is at least two years old.
- Staff and board changes indicate that it's time for the new leaders to create a vision statement of their own.
- So many external or internal factors have changed that the current statement is no longer valid.

If the board has adopted a vision statement within the past year, it may prefer to update or modify the statement rather than create a new one.

Before settling down to the business of developing a vision statement, your organization may want to do a little preparation. You have to find out what your significant stakeholders already think of your organization—that is, talk with people who have a stake in its future. You also must take stock of the organization's history, growth capacity, and resources. You get this information from your stakeholders, including customers or clients, funders, staff, volunteers, and the communities in which you work. This pre-step helps you ground the vision statement in your understanding of what your community expects or wants of you as well as what you have the resources to accomplish.

Often, this preparatory work is done as part of strategic planning, so that the planners can understand the perspectives of people important to the organization. Some nonprofits also choose to follow this step before developing a vision statement. While this is optional, it usually benefits the organization by broadening understanding and ownership of the concepts detailed in the vision.

Find out what significant stakeholders think

The vision statement needs to be in tune with the thinking of significant stakeholders—customers, funders, staff, volunteers, and community. When you consult stakeholders, you are in effect asking them to help define the organization's future; this ensures that the vision statement reflects their opinions and has their support. Because it involves three-to-five-year outcomes, the vision statement must respond quickly to changes in the environment and customers' thinking; stakeholders' opinions are critical in making good decisions quickly.

Your organization can find out what stakeholders think in a number of ways:

- Conduct focus groups with customers, staff, volunteers, and community members.
- Interview policy makers, allies, and competitors.
- Arrange a panel discussion among key informants (individuals who are knowledgeable in an area important to your organization, for example, an expert on funding or what is happening in local government).
- Get information from research reports and evaluation reports.

Consider your organization's history, capacity, and potential resources

Besides knowing the thoughts of your key stakeholders, you need a clear picture of your organization's potential. To sketch a vision that your organization can actually accomplish in three to five years, the leadership has to consider the organization's history, capacity, and potential funding. The organization's history will often play a role in determining its future. Leaders need to have a strong sense of how the organization got where it is so they can make decisions about the logical direction for the immediate future. The current capacity of the organization to compete, grow, serve customers, and represent the community will help pinpoint the role it can play in the future. Leadership will need to consult staff and other key players for their thoughts on the organization's capacity. Finally, the potential the organization has to raise funds and other resources also affects the role it can play in the future. To ascertain potential funding, leadership will need to assess the organization's relationship with funders and get the opinion of fundraisers. Your organization can get this information in several ways:

- *Review your history.* Invite past board members to a meeting to get their perspective on the organization's history. (You can streamline this process by routinely conducting interviews with board members who are leaving the organization. Videotape them reflecting on the organization, so that you have a permanent record.)

- *Assess your capacity.* Hold a staff meeting(s) and ask the staff to identify areas for expansion or contraction and find out if they want to be involved in such changes. Ask managers if anything is keeping them from creating the best future for the community they serve. If something is, determine if the barriers are related to the organization's capacity, internal structure, existing and potential funding, or changing community needs.

- *Contact current and past funders and other resource providers.* Invite fundraisers from other organizations to serve on a panel at a board meeting to discuss the current environment for fundraising to ascertain what's hot and what's not.

Lydia considers the organization's capacity to accomplish its vision.

Compile the results of your background fact finding before creating the vision statement. Write up information on stakeholders' perspectives, history, growth capacity, and potential resources in a *brief* (one-page) form that can be used to inform the vision.

Once you are ready to begin, the six-step process outlined below is effective in developing a vision statement. Use it when creating a vision statement rather than reviewing and updating an existing one.

Step 1: Select the Vision Statement Writing Team

Typically the board chair appoints a writing team of one to three experienced people to be responsible for participating in the board's planning process and then writing the vision statement.

Step 2: Generate Alternative Visions

Working in small groups, participants in the planning process generate viable alternative visions of the future for the community and the organization.

Step 3: Identify Common Themes

Planning participants identify themes that are common to the alternative visions generated in Step 2.

Step 4: Draft the Vision Statement

The vision statement writing team composes the vision statement.

Step 5: Circulate the Vision Statement for Review and Modify It

The writing team circulates the draft of the vision statement to key stakeholders for review, comment, and modification if necessary.

Step 6: Adopt the Vision Statement

The board reviews the vision statement and adopts it for the organization.

Typically, Steps 2 and 3 are done as part of a daylong planning meeting of the planning participants (usually board and key staff or volunteers). If no daylong meeting is planned, schedule two or three planning meetings or complete Steps 2 and 3 during regularly scheduled board meetings. In the appendix at the back of this booklet you will find worksheets to help you develop your vision statement.

Step 1: Select the Vision Statement Writing Team

This step is the same for both the mission statement and the vision statement. Please follow the suggestions given in Part II, Step 1: Select the Mission Statement Writing Team, page 17.

Turn to Vision Worksheet 1: Select the Vision Statement Writing Team, page 57.

Step 2: Generate Alternative Visions

The purpose of this step is for all participants involved in the planning to have an opportunity to envision the future for their community and the organization. This step is often the centerpiece of any strategic planning effort being conducted by the leadership of the organization. Typically the visioning process follows the portion of the meeting where participants have taken a look at where the organization has been and where it is. This analysis takes stock of the organization's Strengths, Weaknesses, Opportunities, Threats, and Mission (SWOTM).

Divide the planning participants (usually the board and key staff and volunteers) into small groups of three to six people each; ideally there will be three or four different groups. (If the planning process includes seven or fewer leaders, they can work as a single unit.) Have each small group appoint a recorder to take notes.

If the facilitator or planning participants have not already done so, they now decide on an approach for generating alternative visions, selecting from the following options. Usually a strategic planning process uses only one option; however, some groups choose to use two. It is important that everyone in the small groups participate in completing the option(s) chosen.

Option A: Critical Issues Approach

Critical issues are problems the organization must resolve if it is to be successful in the future. In this exercise, each small group identifies up to five of the organization's most critical issues and develops a scenario (plan) for solving them within the next three to five years. It will help if the group works in this way:

- Be specific and focused in identifying a problem as a critical issue. For example, "How can we get more funding?" is not specific enough. It should be restated as "How can we become less dependent on United Way support?"

- Do not lump several vexing problems into one critical issue; treat each problem as a separate issue. For example, "How can we recruit, retain, and motivate a more diverse board, staff, and volunteers?" contains several issues and is too broad. Restate it this way: "How can we recruit a more diverse board so that it will reflect the composition of the community that we serve?"

- Frame each critical issue in the form of a question. For example: "How can we serve those families that are no longer covered by welfare and have no current jobs?" "How can we change the identity of the organization from a service provider to an advocacy organization?" "How can we reduce recidivism in our chemical abuse program?"

- Only one critical issue can focus on the problem of getting more money.

- Describe a resolution or desired outcome for each critical issue identified.

- Finally, develop a single scenario that resolves the critical issues. The scenario developed has to answer all the questions the small group identified as critical issues.

After thirty-five to forty-five minutes, each recorder tells the planning participants about the scenario her or his small group developed to answer the organization's critical issues.

Some of the advantages of this approach are that it addresses the big problems facing the organization and very deliberately makes people choose what they will focus on in the future. A disadvantage is that it is problem based and may not capitalize on opportunities or encourage a positive vision of the future.

Option B: News Stories

Each group imagines itself three to five years in the future and develops a news story to describe the organization at that future point. Give the groups paper and pens. The person designated as the small group's recorder plays the part of a newspaper reporter who interviews the organization's board members, played by the rest of the small group. Everyone in the small group must agree to the key points in the news story that comes out of the interviews. The news story should answer the following questions:

- What will be different in the (world, community, or target population) in three to five years because our organization exists?
- What role(s) will our organization play in making this difference?
- Who will be our organization's partners or collaborators in this effort?
- What will our organization be known for in three to five years?

After twenty to twenty-five minutes, each recorder reads her or his small group's news story to the planning participants.

The advantages to this approach are that it is a little more linear for groups that prefer a linear style; also, the news story angle helps participants pick up on specifics and lets them have some fun imagining what a news article in the future might be like. The disadvantage is that some people find it hard to envision significant change when writing the article as if change has already happened.

Option C: Metaphors and Pictures

In this exercise, each group develops a metaphor and drawing that pictures the future three to five years from now. Give each group a sheet of poster board and ten to fifteen colored markers. The instructions are that within two minutes the group will start drawing a picture that is a metaphor for the future. The metaphor should address these questions:

- What will be different in the (world, community, or target population) in three to five years because our organization exists?
- What role(s) will our organization play in making this difference?
- Who will be our organization's partners or collaborators in this effort?
- What will our organization be known for in three to five years?

After twenty to twenty-five minutes, each recorder interprets her or his small group's drawing to all planning participants.

The main advantages to this approach are that it taps into people's intuition, helps them look at the big picture all at once, and is fun, providing a break from the linear approach to planning. The disadvantage is that the details often need to be developed later; there is less information for the writing team to work with.

George, Kim, and Bea present their small groups' drawing to all the planning participants.

Option D: Stakeholders Approach

The planning participants develop a list of the organization's significant stakeholders, such as customers, funders, community members, policy makers, allies, and competitors. Each small group "adopts" one or two stakeholders, with no two groups adopting the same stakeholder(s). Each group assumes the identity of the stakeholder(s) assigned to it and answers the following questions:

- What does the stakeholder think about our organization today?
- What would we like the stakeholder to think and say about us in three to five years?
- What steps does our organization need to take to change our stakeholder's perceptions of us in three to five years?

After twenty-five minutes, each recorder tells the planning participants what her or his small group's stakeholder thinks of the organization now and in three to five years and what changes the organization needs to make to change the stakeholder's perceptions.

The advantages are that this approach is clearly customer focused, allows the different small groups to perceive the organization in different ways simultaneously, and forces people to take off their organization's "hat" and put on a stakeholder's "hat," giving them an opportunity to lose some of their defensiveness. The disadvantage is that the perceptions that emerge are those of stakeholders who have perspectives other than those of the organization's leaders.

There is a separate worksheet for each of the four approaches described above. Depending on the approach (or approaches) the participants selected, distribute the appropriate version of Vision Worksheet 2: Generate Visions, pages 59 to 67.

Step 3: Identify Common Themes

Once the all-important Step 2 is completed, the planning participants need to blend the thinking of the different small groups into one picture. Planning participants first consider all the ideas that were identified in Step 2 and develop a list of common themes—ideas that were presented in at least two to three small group reports. (The common themes should be recorded for the board and key staff for their information and evaluation.) Once the list is complete, the planning group has the opportunity to comment on and modify it so it reflects the thinking of the majority. Here are examples of common themes from one organization:

- The number of homeless people will decline in the future because of our homeowner programs.

- Our organization will play a significant role in raising the community's awareness of the problems of homelessness and what people can do about it.

- We will begin a program to support homeless families who are employed but need transportation and child care to maintain their jobs.

Turn to Vision Worksheet 3: Identify Common Themes, page 67.

Step 4: Draft the Vision Statement

The vision statement writing team bases the vision statement on the common themes generated by the planning group. By generalizing from specific common themes and pushing some key concepts, the team can make the vision statement inspiring and challenging. The key to writing the vision statement is for the team to project itself into the future and then write about the future as if the team were in it.

The vision statement has to focus on outcomes desirable for the community, customers, or both, rather than on outcomes desirable for the organization. Figure 2 shows some examples of organization-centered vision statements that were amended to reflect positive outcomes for customers and the community.

Figure 2: Keep your vision on the customer

From organization focused...	*To customer (or community) focused*
Our organization will expand its programming and become the center for homeless people.	An additional one-hundred homeless families will have shelter for up to thirty nights because of the new center for homeless families.
We will develop transportation and child care programs to support homeless people.	Fifty parents in families in need of transportation and child care in order to maintain their jobs will receive support for up to thirty days a year from the new transportation and child care program.
We will develop the BEST community awareness media program in the Midwest.	The metropolitan community will become more aware of the problems of homelessness and, as a result, will be prepared to support efforts to address these problems.

Distribute Vision Worksheet 4: Draft the Vision Statement, page 69, to the vision statement writing team.

Step 5: Circulate the Vision Statement for Review and Modify It

This step is the same for both the mission statement and the vision statement. Please follow the suggestions given in Part II, Step 6: Circulate the Mission Statement for Review and Modify It, page 23.

Distribute Vision Worksheet 5: Review and Comment on the Vision Statement, page 71, to the people selected for this task.

Step 6: Adopt the Vision Statement

This step is the same for both the mission statement and the vision statement. Please follow the suggestions given in Part II, Step 7: Adopt the Mission Statement, page 23.

Use the adopted vision statement to evaluate the organization's work. The board should review the vision statement at least twice a year to make certain that it and key staff continue to support the statement as written and to weigh how well the organization is achieving its vision. Since the vision statement is considered written in pencil, the board should feel comfortable about making changes as appropriate.

The Leadership Benefits of Crafting Mission and Vision Statements

Clear mission and vision can make miracles happen.

HAVING WORKED with many nonprofit organizations over the years, I have learned that the *process* of developing mission and vision statements is at least as important as the *product.* That's because the process involves the board, key staff, and volunteers in three activities that improve their ability to lead the organization:

- In listening to funders, customers, community, competitors, allies, volunteers, and staff, the leaders begin to make connections to these significant stakeholders and understand them.

- In talking among themselves about the most important issues facing their community and organization, organizational leaders are carrying out their primary responsibility to set the organization's direction.

- In coming to understand each others' thoughts on issues important to the organization, leaders become a team, increasing their collective effectiveness.

It is critical that the leaders of the organization take the time to address its mission and vision statements and communicate them to the staff, volunteers, customers, community, and other stakeholders. If the leaders do not do this, then no one will. Other stakeholders, involved as they are in the day-to-day operation of one area of the organization, simply do not have the outside connections or the breadth of vision required to create an image of the organization's future.

As you begin your work revisiting your organization's mission and envisioning its future, always keep in mind that it is perhaps the most important work that you will do as a leader. But that doesn't mean that the work must be deadly serious; just the opposite. If you can keep the process brief, fun, and nonjudgmental until final decision-making, you will find that the participants are open, enthusiastic, and all the more creative. Remember that the results of these activities are at the very core of why your leaders joined the organization.

All the best as you begin the process of creating your future!

"Wow, this paddling in the same direction really is much easier!"

APPENDIX A

Resources

The Alliance for Nonprofit Management, Alliance web site. See the frequently asked questions (FAQ): "What's in a vision statement?" Available through Internet web site, www.allianceonline.org.

Allison, Michael and Jude Kaye. *Strategic Planning for Nonprofit Organizations: A Practical Guide and Workbook.* New York: John Wiley & Sons, Inc., 1997.

Broholm, Richard R. "The Power and Purpose of Vision in Exemplary Organizations." Boston: Unpublished paper, 1989.

Bryson, John M. *Strategic Planning for Public and Nonprofit Organizations: A Guide to Strengthening and Sustaining Organizational Achievement,* 2nd Edition. San Francisco: Jossey-Bass, 1995.

Bryson, John M. and Farnum K. Alston. *Creating and Implementing Your Strategic Plan: A Workbook for Public and Nonprofit Organizations.* San Francisco: Jossey-Bass, 1995.

California Management Assistance Partnership, Nonprofit Genie web site. See the following frequently asked questions (FAQ): "Why Plan?" "How Much Time and Money Does It Take to Do Strategic Planning?" "What Does a Typical Planning Process Look Like?" "What Is the Difference Between a Mission and a Purpose?" Available through Internet web site, www.genie.org.

Carver, John. *Boards That Make a Difference.* San Francisco: Jossey-Bass, 1990.

The Drucker Foundation for Nonprofit Management. *The Drucker Foundation Self-Assessment Tool for Nonprofit Organizations.* San Francisco: Jossey-Bass, 1993.

Hummel, Joan M. *Starting and Running a Nonprofit Organization,* 2nd Edition. Minneapolis: University of Minnesota Press, 1996.

Sharken Simon, Judith. *The Fieldstone Alliance Nonprofit Guide to Conducting Successful Focus Groups: How to Get the Information You Need to Make Smart Decisions.* St. Paul: Fieldstone Alliance, 1999.

Stern, Gary J. *Marketing Workbook for Nonprofit Organizations Volume 1: Develop the Plan,* 2nd Edition. St. Paul: Fieldstone Alliance, 2001.

Winer, Michael and Karen Ray. *Collaboration Handbook: Creating, Sustaining, and Enjoying the Journey.* St. Paul: Fieldstone Alliance, 1994.

APPENDIX B

Worksheets

This worksheet will help you identify a mission statement writing team and develop a charge for the team.

1. Identify one to three people from the board, staff, and volunteers. The team might include formal and informal leaders, people committed to involvement in the planning process, and individuals with marketing and writing skills.

   a._____   (TeamLeader)

   b._____

   c._____

2. Write a brief charge for the committee. This might include the following:

   Review the current mission statement and decide if it needs to be rewritten.

   Write the mission statement for the organization, including core values and underlying strategies.

   Give the board at least two drafts of the new mission statement.

   Charge:

3. Identify a due date for the team: _____

This worksheet will help the planning participants identify value statements that are important to them and to the organization. It can be used by each participant, by small group recorders, or by both. The final list of values should be given to the mission statement writing team.

Identify your organization's core values. These include beliefs central to your organization, those that your organization considers most important. Avoid one-word platitudes; be as specific as possible.

List the values here:

This worksheet will help you identify the underlying strategies (methods, approaches) that your organization uses to accomplish its mission.

If there is a current list of underlying strategies, list the top three or four below. If no list of underlying strategies exists, create one. Using your organization's programs and services as a jumping-off point, identify the underlying or general strategies that the organization uses to accomplish its mission. Limit your list to three or four statements.

A.

B.

C.

D.

This worksheet will help the planning participants evaluate the current mission statement by responding to the questions below. It can be used by each participant, by small group recorders, or by both. The results should be given to the mission statement writing team.

1. Write the current mission statement:

2. Is the current mission statement short and snappy? If not, what is the problem?

3. Does it tell people what good the organization is doing and for whom? If not, what is missing, or is too much included?

4. Is it grounded in our values as clarified in Step 2? If not, what is missing? (Remember, though, that the mission statement should not be a *list* of your values. It needs to capture their essence without being muddied up by a long list.)

5. Does the statement serve as an umbrella that covers all the things we do—our underlying strategies as captured in Step 3? If not, what is not included under the umbrella?

6. Does the statement encompass all the people to whom we target our services? If not, which customers are missing?

7. Does the statement communicate who we are to the average person? If not, why not? For example, does it have too much jargon? Is it unclear or too abstract?

8. Is this a statement we can get excited about and be proud of? If not, what must be done?

This worksheet will help the mission statement writing team write at least two drafts of the mission statement for the board.

Write a one-sentence mission statement that clarifies the purpose of the organization. Answer the following questions to help you identify the ideas to be included in the statement.

1. What good (what outcome) is the organization trying to achieve? Try to come up with an umbrella statement.

2. For whom are we trying to accomplish the good or outcomes? Try to come up with one target population.

This worksheet will help you get input from key stakeholders on the draft mission statement. Circulate the draft statement and ask people to answer these questions about it.

Write the new mission statement here:

1. Do you understand the mission statement? If not, explain.

2. Does it fit your experiences with our organization? If not, explain.

3. Do you like this statement as a mission for our organization? If not, explain.

This worksheet will help you identify a vision statement writing team and develop a charge for the team.

1. Identify one to three people from the board, staff, and volunteers. The team might include formal and informal leaders, people committed to involvement in the planning process, and individuals with marketing and writing skills.

   a._____   (TeamLeader)

   b._____

   c._____

2. Write a brief charge for the committee. This might include the following:

   • Review the current vision statement and decide if it needs to be rewritten.
   • Write the vision statement for the organization.
   • Give the board at least two drafts of the new vision statement.

   Charge:

3. Identify a due date for the team: _____

This worksheet will help the planning participants outline draft vision statements.

1. Participants should identify no more than five critical issues the organization faces. Frame critical issues in the form of a question. Below each issue, briefly describe a way to resolve the problem.

   Critical Issue 1:

   Resolution:

   Critical Issue 2:

   Resolution:

   Critical Issue 3:

   Resolution:

   Critical Issue 4:

   Resolution:

   Critical Issue 5:

   Resolution:

2. Write one scenario for the future that addresses all the critical issues identified.

This worksheet will help the planning participants outline draft vision statements.

After completing the visioning exercise, participants should answer the following questions:

1. What will be different in the (world, community, or target population) in three to five years because our organization exists?

2. What role(s) will our organization play in making this difference?

3. Who will be our organization's partners or collaborators in this effort?

4. What will our organization be known for in three to five years?

This worksheet will help the planning participants outline draft vision statements.

After completing the visioning exercise, participants should answer the following questions:

1. What will be different in the (world, community, or target population) in three to five years because our organization exists?

2. What role(s) will our organization play in making this difference?

3. Who will be our organization's partners or collaborators in this effort?

4. What will our organization be known for in three to five years?

This worksheet will help the planning participants outline draft vision statements.

After completing the visioning exercise, participants should answer the following questions:

1. What does the stakeholder think about our organization today?

2. What would we like the stakeholder to think and say about us in three to five years?

3. What steps does our organization need to take to change our stakeholder's perceptions of us in three to five years?

This worksheet will help you identify common themes from those compiled by the small groups during the visioning process. If you are working with several small groups of participants, you can consider common themes as those stated in a majority of the small groups' visions.

List the common themes that the small groups identified in Step 2: Generate Alternative Visions:

1.

2.

3.

4.

5.

6.

7.

8.

Working with the suggestions presented in Step 4: Draft the Vision Statement, the writing team can use this worksheet to develop at least two drafts of the vision statement for the board.

This worksheet will help you get input from key stakeholders on the draft vision statement. Circulate the draft statement and ask people to answer these questions about it.

1. Do you understand the vision statement? If not, explain.

2. Does it fit your experiences with our organization? If not, explain.

3. Do you like this statement as a vision for our organization? If not, explain.

More results-oriented books from Fieldstone Alliance

Boards

The Best of the Board Café
Hands-on Solutions for Nonprofit Boards

by Jan Masaoka, CompassPoint Nonprofit Services

Gathers the most requested articles from the e-newsletter, *Board Café*. You'll find a lively menu of ideas, information, opinions, news, and resources to help board members give and get the most out of their board service.

232 pp • Item 069407 • ISBN 978-0-940069-40-4

The Nonprofit Board Member's Guide to Lobbying and Advocacy

by Marcia Avner

Board members are uniquely positioned to be effective and influential lobbyists. This guide spells out how your board can use their power and privilege to move your nonprofit's work forward.

128 pp • Item 069393 • ISBN 978-0-940069-39-8

Collaboration

Collaboration Handbook
Creating, Sustaining, and Enjoying the Journey

by Michael Winer and Karen Ray

Shows you how to get a collaboration going, set goals, determine everyone's roles, create an action plan, and evaluate the results. Includes a case study of one collaboration from start to finish, helpful tips on how to avoid pitfalls, and worksheets to keep everyone on track.

192 pp • Item 069032 • ISBN 978-0-940069-03-9

Collaboration: What Makes It Work, 2nd Ed.
by Paul Mattessich, PhD, Marta Murray-Close, BA, and Barbara Monsey, MPH

An in-depth review of current collaboration research. Major findings are summarized, critical conclusions are drawn, and twenty key factors influencing successful collaborations are identified. Includes *The Wilder Collaboration Factors Inventory*, which groups can use to assess their collaboration.

104 pp • Item 069326 • ISBN 978-0-940069-32-9

The Nimble Collaboration
Fine-Tuning Your Collaboration for Lasting Success

by Karen Ray

Shows you ways to make your existing collaboration more responsive, flexible, and productive. Provides three key strategies to help your collaboration respond quickly to changing environments and participants.

136 pp • Item 069288 • ISBN 978-0-940069-28-2

Community Building

Community Building: What Makes It Work
by Wilder Research Center

Reveals twenty-eight keys to help you build community more effectively. Includes detailed descriptions of each factor, case examples of how they play out, and practical questions to assess your work.

112 pp • Item 069121 • ISBN 978-0-940069-12-1

The Community Economic Development Handbook
Strategies and Tools to Revitalize Your Neighborhood

by Mihailo Temali

A concrete, practical handbook to turning any neighborhood around. It explains how to start a community economic development organization, and then lays out the steps of four proven and powerful strategies for revitalizing inner-city neighborhoods.

288 pp • Item 069369 • ISBN 978-0-940069-36-7

Visit **www.FieldstoneAlliance.org** to learn more about these and many other books on community building, nonprofit management, and funder capacity. You can also sign up to receive our free "Tools You Can Use" e-newsletter and find out about our consulting services. Call 1-800-274-6024 for a current catalog.

Community Leadership Handbook
Framing Ideas, Building Relationships, and Mobilizing Resources

by James F. Krile with Gordon Curphy and Duane R. Lund

Leadership is a choice, not a position. You can improve your community, and this hands-on guide shows you how. Based on the best of Blandin Foundation's 20-year experience in developing community leaders, it gives community members—like yourself—the tools to bring people together to make changes.

216 pp • Item 069547 • ISBN 978-0-940069-54-1

The Fieldstone Alliance Nonprofit Field Guide to Conducting Community Forums

by Carol Lukas and Linda Hoskins

Provides step-by-step instruction to plan and carry out exciting, successful community forums that will educate the public, build consensus, focus action, or influence policy.

128 pp • Item 069318 • ISBN 978-0-940069-31-2

The Creative Community Builder's Handbook
How to Transform Communities Using Local Assets, Arts, and Culture

by Tom Borrup

Art and culture can be a powerful catalyst for revitalizing the economic, social, and physical conditions in communities. This handbook gives you successful strategies, best practices, and "how-to" guidance to turn cultural gems into effective community change.

280 pp • Item 069474 • ISBN 978-0-940069-47-3

Crossing Borders, Sharing Journeys
Effective Capacity Building with Immigrant and Refugee Groups

by Sarah Gleason

This report outlines seven broad factors found to contribute to effective capacity building with immigrant and refugee lead organizations (IRLOs). Case studies illustrate practices used when working with IRLOs and highlights principles that other capacity builders can apply when working with similar groups. You can also download a free copy of this report at www.FieldstoneAlliance.org.

88 pp • Item 069628 • ISBN 978-0-940069-62-6

New Americans, New Promise
A Guide to the Refugee Journey in America

by Yorn Yan

Gain a better understanding of the refugee experience in the U.S. Refugee-serving organizations will find solid, practical advice for how to best help refugees through the acculturation and transition process of becoming a New American. Refugees will discover what to expect during five stages of development that they typically progress through as they adapt to their new home.

200 pp • Item 069504 • ISBN 978-0-940069-50-3

Finance

Bookkeeping Basics
What Every Nonprofit Bookkeeper Needs to Know

by Debra L. Ruegg and Lisa M. Venkatrathnam

Complete with step-by-step instructions, a glossary of accounting terms, detailed examples, and handy reproducible forms, this book will enable you to successfully meet the basic bookkeeping requirements of your nonprofit organization—even if you have little or no formal accounting training.

128 pp • Item 069296 • ISBN 978-0-940069-29-9

Coping with Cutbacks
The Nonprofit Guide to Success When Times Are Tight

by Emil Angelica and Vincent Hyman

Shows you practical ways to involve business, government, and other nonprofits to solve problems together. Also includes 185 cutback strategies you can put to use right away.

128 pp • Item 069091 • ISBN 978-0-940069-09-1

Financial Leadership for Nonprofit Executives
Guiding Your Organization to Long-term Success

by Jeanne Bell and Elizabeth Schaffer

Gives the Executive Director the framework, specific language, and processes needed to lead with confidence and create an effective nonprofit business that strikes the balance between mission and money.

152 pp • Item 06944X • ISBN 978-0-940069-44-2

Venture Forth!
The Essential Guide to Starting a Moneymaking Business in Your Nonprofit Organization

by Rolfe Larson

The most complete guide on nonprofit business development. Building on the experience of dozens of organizations, this handbook gives you a time-tested approach for finding, testing, and launching a successful nonprofit business venture.

272 pp • Item 069245 • ISBN 978-0-940069-24-4

Funder's Guides

Community Visions, Community Solutions
Grantmaking for Comprehensive Impact

by Joseph A. Connor and Stephanie Kadel-Taras

Helps foundations, community funds, government agencies, and other grantmakers uncover a community's highest aspiration for itself, and support and sustain strategic efforts to get to workable solutions.

128 pp • Item 06930X • ISBN 978-0-940069-30-5

A Funder's Guide to Evaluation
Leveraging Evaluation to Improve Nonprofit Effectiveness

by Peter York

Shifts away from using evaluation to prove something to someone else, and toward improving what nonprofits do so they can achieve their mission and share how they succeeded with others.

160 pp • Item 069482 • ISBN 978-0-940069-48-0

A Funder's Guide to Organizational Assessment
Tools, Processes, and Their Use in Building Capacity

Editor: Lori Bartczak

Funders, grantees, and consultants will understand how organizational assessment can be used to 1) Build the capacity of nonprofits, 2) Enhance grantmaking, 3) Impact organizational systems, 4) Strengthen the nonprofit sector, and 5) Measure foundation effectiveness. The guide presents four grantee assessment tools and two tools for assessing foundation performance.

216 pp • Item 069539 • ISBN 978-0-940069-53-4
Includes CD-ROM with examples and adaptations of tools

Power in Policy
A Funder's Guide to Advocacy and Civic Participation

Editor: David F. Arons

Increasingly, foundations are finding that participation in public decision making is often a critical component in reaching the impact demanded by mission-related goals. For those weighing precisely what role foundations should play, the mix of real-life examples, practical advice, and inspiration in this book are invaluable.

320 pp • Item 069458 • ISBN 978-0-940069-45-9

Strengthening Nonprofit Performance
A Funder's Guide to Capacity Building

by Paul Connolly and Carol Lukas

This practical guide synthesizes the most recent capacity building practice and research into a collection of strategies, steps, and examples that you can use to get started on or improve funding to strengthen nonprofit organizations.

176 pp • Item 069377 • ISBN 978-0-940069-37-4

Lobbing, Advocacy, and Organizing

The Lobbying and Advocacy Handbook for Nonprofit Organizations
Shaping Public Policy at the State and Local Level

by Marcia Avner

The Lobbying and Advocacy Handbook is a planning guide and resource for nonprofit organizations that want to influence issues that matter to them. This book will help you decide whether to lobby and then put plans in place to make it work.

240 pp • Item 069261 • ISBN 978-0-940069-26-8

The Nonprofit Board Member's Guide to Lobbying and Advocacy
by Marcia Avner

Written specifically for board members, this guide helps organizations increase their impact on policy decisions. It reveals how board members can be involved in planning for and implementing successful lobbying efforts.

96 pp • Item 069393 • ISBN 978-0-940069-39-8

Management & Planning

The Accidental Techie
Supporting, Managing, and Maximizing Your Nonprofit's Technology

by Sue Bennett

How to support and manage technology on a day-to-day basis including: setting up a help desk, developing an effective technology budget and implementation plan, working with consultants and management, handling viruses, creating a backup system and schedule, purchasing hardware and software, and more.

176 pp • Item 069490 • ISBN 978-0-940069-49-7

Benchmarking for Nonprofits
How to Measure, Manage, and Improve Performance

by Jason Saul

Benchmarking is the continuous process of measuring your organization against leaders to gain knowledge and insights that will help you improve. This book defines a formal, systematic, and reliable way to benchmark—from preparing your organization to measuring performance and implementing best practices.

144 pp • Item 069431 • ISBN 978-0-940069-43-5

Consulting with Nonprofits
A Practitioner's Guide

by Carol A. Lukas

A step-by-step, comprehensive guide for consultants. Addresses the art of consulting, how to run your business, and much more. Also includes tips and anecdotes from thirty skilled consultants.

240 pp • Item 069172 • ISBN 978-0-940069-17-6

The Fieldstone Alliance Nonprofit Field Guide to
Developing Effective Teams

by Beth Gilbertsen and Vijit Ramchandani

Helps you understand, start, and maintain a team. Provides tools and techniques for writing a mission statement, setting goals, conducting effective meetings, creating ground rules to manage team dynamics, making decisions in teams, creating project plans, and developing team spirit.

80 pp • Item 069202 • ISBN 978-0-940069-20-6

The Five Life Stages of Nonprofit Organizations
Where You Are, Where You're Going, and What to Expect When You Get There

by Judith Sharken Simon with J. Terence Donovan

Shows you what's "normal" for each development stage which helps you plan for transitions, stay on track, and avoid unnecessary struggles. Includes *The Nonprofit Life Stage Assessment* to plot your organization's progress in seven arenas of organization development.

128 pp • Item 069229 • ISBN 978-0-940069-22-0

Generations
The Challenge of a Lifetime for Your Nonprofit

by Peter Brinckerhoff

What happens when a management team of all Baby Boomers leaves within a five-year stretch? The clock is ticking . . . . is your nonprofit ready? In this book, nonprofit mission expert Peter Brinckerhoff tells you what generational changes to expect and how to plan for them. You'll find in-depth information for each area of your organization—staff, board, volunteers, clients, marketing, technology, and finances.

232 pp • Item 069555 • ISBN 978-0-940069-55-8

Information Gold Mine
Innovative Uses of Evaluation

by Paul W. Mattessich, Shelly Hendricks, Ross VeLure Roholt

Don't underestimate the power of your evaluation findings. The real-life stories in this book clearly show the power of using evaluation data to produce good things for your nonprofit.

128 pp • Item 069512 • ISBN 978-0-940069-51-0

The Manager's Guide to Program Evaluation:
Planning, Contracting, and Managing for Useful Results

by Paul W. Mattessich, Ph.D.

Explains how to plan and manage an evaluation that will help identify your organization's successes, share information with key audiences, and improve services.

96 pp • Item 069385 • ISBN 978-0-940069-38-1

The Nonprofit Mergers Workbook Part I
The Leader's Guide to Considering, Negotiating, and Executing a Merger

by David La Piana

Save time, money, and untold frustration with this highly practical guide that makes the merger process manageable and controllable. Includes case studies, decision trees, twenty-two worksheets, checklists, tips, and complete step-by-step guidance.

240 pp • Item 069210 • ISBN 978-0-940069-21-3

The Nonprofit Mergers Workbook Part II
Unifying the Organization after a Merger

by La Piana Associates

Once the merger agreement is signed, the question becomes: How do we make this merger work? *Part II* helps you create a comprehensive plan to achieve *integration*—bringing together people, programs, processes, and systems from two (or more) organizations into a single, unified whole.

248 pp • Item 069415 • ISBN 978-0-940069-41-1
Includes CD-ROM with integration plan template

Nonprofit Stewardship
A Better Way to Lead Your Mission-Based Organization

by Peter Brinckerhoff

This guide outlines eight characteristics of a mission-based steward and gives you specific applications of stewardship—in planning and finance, risk-taking, and crisis management.

272 pp • Item 069423 • ISBN 978-0-940069-42-8

Resolving Conflict in Nonprofit Organizations
The Leader's Guide to Finding Constructive Solutions

by Marion Peters Angelica

Learn and practice conflict resolution skills, uncover and deal with the true issues, and design and conduct a conflict resolution process.

192 pp • Item 069164 • ISBN 978-0-940069-16-9

Strategic Planning Workbook for Nonprofit Organizations, Revised and Updated

by Bryan Barry

Chart a wise course for your nonprofit's future. This time-tested workbook gives you practical step-by-step guidance, real-life examples, and easy-to-use worksheets.

120 pp • Item 069075 • ISBN 978-0-940069-07-7
Includes CD-ROM with worksheets and templates

Marketing & Fundraising

The Fieldstone Alliance Nonprofit Field Guide to
Conducting Successful Focus Groups

by Judith Sharken Simon

Shows how to collect valuable information without a lot of money or special expertise. Using this proven technique, you'll get essential opinions and feedback to help you check out your assumptions, do better strategic planning, improve services or products, and more.

80 pp • Item 069199 • ISBN 978-0-940069-19-0

Marketing Workbook for Nonprofit Organizations
Volume I: Develop the Plan

by Gary J. Stern

Don't just wish for results—get them! Here's how to create a straightforward, usable marketing plan. Includes the six Ps of Marketing, how to use them effectively, a sample marketing plan, tips on using the Internet, and worksheets.

208 pp • Item 069253 • ISBN 978-0-940069-25-1

Marketing Workbook for Nonprofit Organizations
Volume II: Mobilize People for Marketing Success

by Gary J. Stern

Put together a successful promotional campaign based on the most persuasive tool of all: personal contact. Learn how to mobilize your entire organization, its staff, volunteers, and supporters in a focused, one-to-one marketing campaign.

192 pp • Item 069105 • ISBN 978-0-940069-10-7

Message Matters
Succeeding at the Crossroads of Mission and Market

by Rebecca Leet

Today, being heard demands delivering information that resonates with your audience's desires quickly, clearly, and continually. Message Matters gives you a simple framework for developing and using strategic messages so you can connect more successfully with your target audiences and compel them to action.

160 pp • Item 069636 • ISBN 978-0-940069-63-3

Ordering Information

  Call toll-free: 800-274-6024
Internationally: 651-556-4509

 Fax: 651-556-4517

E-mail: books@fieldstonealliance.org
Online: www.FieldstoneAlliance.org

Pricing and discounts

For current prices and discounts, please visit our web site at www.FieldstoneAlliance.org or call toll free at 800-274-6024.

Our NO-RISK guarantee

If you aren't completely satisfied with any book for any reason, simply send it back within 30 days for a full refund.

Quality assurance

We strive to make sure that all the books we publish are helpful and easy to use. Our major workbooks are tested and critiqued by experts before being published. Their comments help shape the final book and—we trust—make it more useful to you.

Do you have a book idea?

Fieldstone Alliance seeks manuscripts and proposals for books in the fields of nonprofit management and community development. To get a copy of our author guidelines, please call us at 800-274-6024. You can also download them from our web site at www.FieldstoneAlliance.org

Visit us online

You'll find information about Fieldstone Alliance and more details on our books, such as table of contents, pricing, discounts, endorsements, and more, at www.FieldstoneAlliance.org.

CPSIA information can be obtained
at www.ICGtesting.com
Printed in the USA
BVHW011225241019
561979BV00010B/962/P